Original title:
Ode to the Oldest Oak

Copyright © 2025 Creative Arts Management OÜ
All rights reserved.

Author: Henry Beaumont
ISBN HARDBACK: 978-1-80567-338-5
ISBN PAPERBACK: 978-1-80567-637-9

Boughs that Touch the Shadows

Beneath the mighty limbs so wide,
Squirrels store nuts with quite the pride.
While birds hold conferences up high,
All the secrets that they can't deny.

Old Oak chuckles in the breeze,
'These critters think they're hard to please!'
With each little rustle and every sway,
Nature's comedians put on a play.

A Serene Witness to Change

Years roll by in a curious dance,
Watching the seasons take their chance.
From budding blooms to autumn's dust,
Old Oak shrugs, 'In nature, we trust!'

Humans pass, dressed in their best,
With selfies aplenty, no time to rest.
But Old Oak leans, a knowing grin,
'I've seen better styles, where have you been?'

The Canopy's Embrace

In summer's warmth, the shade he gives,
A picnic spot where laughter lives.
While ants march off, a steadfast crew,
Old Oak quips, 'I've got work to do!'

When autumn leaves begin to fall,
He teases friends, 'Not done with brawl!'
Gather around, don't miss the fun,
Watch as squirrels compete for a bun!

Silhouettes of Yesterday's Dreams

Once a sapling, small and spry,
Now a giant reaching the sky.
With tales of storms and games of hide,
Old Oak laughs, 'I'm not even tried!'

The kids who once climbed my thighs,
Now play under different skies.
But every shadow tells a tale,
Of dreams that dance in breezes pale.

The Crown of Green Majesty

In the forest, tall and wide,
Sits a tree with leafy pride,
Worn out hat made of moss,
Calls the squirrels, 'Come, be my boss!'

Raccoons hide in its shadow,
As the chipmunks dance below,
Branches scratch like a bad beard,
'Hairy tree!'—its bark cheers weird.

Guardianship of the Age

Guarding old secrets, whispered low,
Rainy days, it turns to glow,
With each gust, it shakes and sways,
'No, not the squirrels, hide the lays!'

Mighty trunk, a fortress stance,
Bravely offers shade for prance,
"Grandpa Oak, we're here for tales!"
Then snickers echo through the gales.

An Abode for Woodland Spirits

Home for fairies, true and spry,
With tiny wings that flutter by,
They sip on dew like fancy tea,
'Don't mind the acorns, just let them be!'

A gnome stands guard by roots so stout,
Holding dreams, without a doubt,
'Watch the birds!' he shouts with glee,
'We've got a front-row view with free!'

Stories of Shelter and Sunlight

Underneath, the sunlight beams,
Shadows dance on laughter's dreams,
Every leaf a tale to spin,
'Gather 'round, let's now begin!'

The owls chuckle, night is near,
Bats fly by with vibrant cheer,
"This old fellow's wise and sweet,
But scraps his jokes—he's lost his light!"

The Dance of Shadows Beneath

In summer's heat, the shadows sway,
The squirrels plan a grand ballet.
Branches twist in a comical way,
While birds shout cheers, 'Hip-hip-hooray!'

Each gust of wind brings a new beat,
Leaves join in, tapping tiny feet.
Who knew the trees could be so neat?
Nature's stage, quite the treat!

Each Ring a Year, Each Year a Tale

With every ring, a birthday cheer,
Old Oak chuckles, 'Bring me beer!'
Each layer tells of jokes and play,
Of acorn parties in the hay.

As seasons passed, he grew quite wise,
Spinning yarns that could mesmerize.
'Remember when the wind was sly?',
He'd wink and say with a twinkling eye.

Timeless Wisdom in Twisting Branches

With branches that twist like a funky dance,
Old Oak shares secrets at every chance.
'Don't eat yellow leaves!' he'll kindly state,
While critters giggle, they won't be late.

He's seen it all, the good and bad,
From storms of rage to merry lad.
'Just sway and bend,' he often hums,
'And laugh at troubles, they'll turn to crumbs.'

Legacy of Lush Embrace

In the embrace of lush green arms,
Old Oak protects from all alarms.
"Stay a while, don't rush away!"
He beckons critters to come and play.

With roots so deep, he tells the ground,
'Respect my wisdom, it knows no bound.'
He guards the laughter, joy's sweet grace,
As kids make memories in his space.

Canopy Dreams and Sunlit Gleams

In the shade, squirrels conspire,
Plotting snacks to build their empire.
While branches sway with a creaky song,
The old oak chuckles, 'You won't last long!'

With leaves like confetti, a party awaits,
Dancing in breezes, throwing up states.
While shadows play tag with the light,
The oak just snickers, 'I've seen it all, right?'

Life Etched in Layers of Green

Each ring in the trunk tells tales so bold,
Of acorns lost and friendships sold.
Bugs throw barbecues without a care,
While the woodpecker plays punk rock flair.

Grass grows beneath like a wild parade,
While rabbits hop in their leafy charade.
The oak laughs softly, 'You've got no sprout,
But the roots know secrets, that's what it's about!'

The Old Oak's Embrace at Dusk

As dusk falls, the parties ignite,
Crickets jump in their evening delight.
'Just sit tight,' the oak softly beams,
'I'm the best seat for your wildest dreams.'

With laughter in rings and moonlight chores,
Woodpeckers knock on imaginary doors.
'Come join the fun!' the branches proclaim,
'Though I'm never called by my real name!'

A Home for Every Creature's Story

In my limbs, there's a cozy home,
For raccoons, owls, and a curious gnome.
They gather for meetings, who would have guessed?
To decide if the leaves or acorns are best!

The squirrels crew up, with plans that won't quit,
While the insects plot a caffeinated skit.
'Imagine my life, it's a true comedy!
But watch your head; don't disturb my serenity!'

Whispers of the Woodland Sage

In the forest where squirrels do prance,
Stands a wise tree with a curious stance.
It sways to the rhythm of critters in glee,
Chattering secrets of life by decree.

With leaves like confetti, it chuckles aloud,
A grandparent figure, eternally proud.
Telling tall tales of the days gone by,
While mushrooms laugh softly, oh my, oh my!

Our Roots Together

Two roots intertwined, a comedic sight,
Thoroughly tangled in a goofy fight.
They argue and bicker, about sun and rain,
While worms wiggle by, grinning in vain.

The acorns chuckle, falling from high,
Wishing they'd landed straight up in the sky.
But together they grow, strong as can be,
A duo of mischief, a roots jubilee!

Timeless Majesty

Behold the ancient giant that sways,
With branches of wisdom, and lots of play.
He dons a crown made of leaves, oh so grand,
Performing a dance, but only on command!

The owl mocks him, while perched on a limb,
Singing a tune with a dance so grim.
Yet each time he shakes, the whole forest quakes,
And laughter erupts from the ground as it shakes!

Nature's Crown

A jester with acorns, the oldest around,
Hiding surprises deep underground.
His branches provide shade for a game of tag,
While chipmunks scamper, they giggle and brag.

He's seen it all from where he stands tall,
A ruler of mischief with laughter for all.
In his crown made of leaves, there's a story to tell,
Of nature's big show, and a tree that's quite swell!

In the Shadow of the Ancient

Beneath the great tree, the chatter is loud,
With critters convened, forming their crowd.
A game of charades in the shade of his trunk,
While the old sage nods, puffing out his funk.

A squirrel steals a nut, the crowd bursts in cheer,
While the old tree rolls eyes, "Oh dear, oh dear!"
Yet in all the laughter, there's wisdom we find,
In the shadow of ages, camaraderie twined.

The Canopy's Breath in Stillness

In quiet shade where squirrels play,
The ancient oak holds secrets gay.
With branches wide, it looks so wise,
Yet drops a limb when laughter flies.

A sturdy trunk, so strong and stout,
Once served as base for kids' grand scout.
Now it just sighs, 'No more tree forts!'
As pigeons perch and plan their sorts.

Old Roots, New Horizons

Deep down below, the roots do stretch,
Like wrinkled hands, they firmly fetch.
Old stories told in whispers low,
Yet young ones sprout, eager to grow.

In summer's heat, they dance and sway,
While acorns plan their grand ballet.
The old oak grins, it knows the tune,
That life goes on, from sun to moon.

Whispers of Leaves in the Breeze

The leaves gossip in various tones,
While critters plot their little moans.
An acorn slips, it hits the ground,
And starts a tale that spins around.

With every gust, a chuckle soars,
As branches knock like playful doors.
'Who'd thought I'd stand and witness fun?'
The oak just laughs, 'I've just begun!'

Life's Stories Inscribed in Bark

Each carved heart and initial rhyme,
Tells youthful tales of puppy love's prime.
With every marking, memories seep,
While smart squirrels plot and never sleep.

Old wood holds laughter, some tears too,
Collecting moments, both old and new.
It chuckles gently, 'I'll stand and see,
Just what these nuts decide to be.'

The Dance of Life Beneath the Boughs

Beneath your branches, critters play,
Squirrels dance, hip-hop all day.
Rabbits prance in silly shoes,
While the worms groove to their blues.

A parade of ants marches by,
In tiny hats, oh my, oh my!
Your trunk, a stage for comic acts,
Nature's laugh, with silly facts.

Raindrops tap like a playful band,
While birds sing as if they've planned.
Under your watch, it's quite a show,
Life's a circus, don't you know?

So here's to you, old friend so spry,
With branches raised, reaching for the sky.
In this funny dance, we all partake,
With you, dear tree, the best of mates.

The Legacy of the Living Sentinels

You're a giant tree, we all agree,
With tales of youth, oh, what glee!
Your bark, a story, full of cracks,
With every ring, a laugh that stacks.

The squirrels chatter, wise and bold,
Reciting secrets from times of old.
Your shade is where the gossip flies,
As the breeze carries garden lies.

A nest of birds, they squawk and tease,
About the time you lost some leaves.
With each breeze, they jest and cheer,
Celebrating life year after year.

Oh, living sentinel, tall and grand,
You hold the joy of this fine land.
Your legacy, a giggling spree,
Where every laugh belongs to thee.

Recollections of a Slow-Growing Heart

In your shadow, time crawls slow,
Like sloths on branches, taking it slow.
Each year a ring, a slow reveal,
Of whispered jokes, it feels so real.

You're aged and wise, but not so spry,
With a funky branch that waves "hello" high.
The memories dance like leaves in fall,
In your embrace, we're having a ball.

With each new leaf, a giggle shared,
Of summer heat, and how you dared.
To spread your arms, and gather friends,
Where laughter and twilight never ends.

So here's your heart, a treasure slow,
In laughter's current, we all flow.
A slow-growing tale of funny delight,
Beneath your boughs, the world feels right.

The Old Guardian's Night Watch

As dusk descends, you stand so tall,
A guardian bold, overseeing all.
With stars above in a twinkling spree,
You chuckle softly, just like me.

The fireflies light the evening dance,
In your shadow, they take a chance.
They wink and blink, a sparkly show,
While owls hoot your jokes, nice and low.

You bob your branches, giggling with glee,
As raccoons play their nightly spree.
In the moonlight, the laughter soars,
The old guardian opens up his doors.

With every creak, you share a tale,
Of nightly mischief, keen and frail.
Oh trusty tree, through laughter complete,
You guard the night with humor sweet.

The Age of Twisted Branches

In a world where branches dance and sway,
An ancient oak claims its feathery sway.
Old age sits high upon its crown,
While squirrels plot tricks in leafy gown.

Its bark tells tales, both bold and bright,
Of acorns lost in glorious flight.
With knots like laughter, gnarled and spry,
It plays peekaboo with the cloudy sky.

The roots are deep, like bedtime snore,
Yet wooden limbs wave, 'Come, explore!'
Birds chirp secrets, with a grin so wide,
As the oak chuckles, filled with pride.

Under this king, the shade is grand,
With shadowy stories at every hand.
Bring your picnic, let laughter soar,
For in this haven, we all want more.

Seasons Crafted in Bark

Leaves have come and leaves have gone,
Yet the oak stands proud, a timeless dawn.
Its branches stretch like old man's hands,
Reaching out for the fun that life demands.

Winter comes with frosty breath,
But the oak stays bold, defying death.
Snowballs fly from its sturdy arms,
As the kids giggle at winter charms.

Spring arrives dressed in colors bright,
With pollen dances in plain sight.
Bees buzz by in a frisky race,
While the oak just smiles, a wise old face.

Summer brings the sun's hot glare,
But the oak spreads shade, that's only fair.
Impromptu naps and picnics unfold,
In its embrace, life's stories told.

A Reverie Underneath the Old Giant

Beneath the giant, dreams take flight,
With roots like dragons in the night.
Picnic ants march like tiny troops,
While the oak chuckles and watches the loops.

Thoughts drift like clouds in playful chase,
Where a squirrel steals an old hat's place.
Laughter echoes in the breeze so light,
As leaves clap hands in pure delight.

Kids lie back, counting green and gold,
While the oak winks, feeling bold.
A throne of nature, it softly sighs,
As secrets rustle with every guise.

A napping dog steals all the show,
Dreaming wild of chasing a crow.
Under this sage, sweet dreams run free,
The old giant fosters joy endlessly.

The Echo of Nature's Legacy

Time has whispered to the oak so wise,
Crafting stories in its weathered guise.
With every ring, a memory stored,
Of curious creatures that once adored.

In autumn's gold, leaves take a dive,
While the oak links arms with the jiving thrive.
With every rustle, it shakes a grin,
Whispering tales of where it's been.

Nature's laughter sings through the air,
As woodpeckers tap two-step with flair.
It boasts of weather, from storms to calm,
In every twist, lies nature's charm.

So raise a toast to this wooden knight,
A guardian of day and cozy night.
With humor woven in every crack,
The oak is alive, no looking back.

Shades of Memory

In the shade of green delight,
An acorn tried to take flight.
But gravity's a heavy prince,
And it just sat, not convinced.

The squirrels call it wise and old,
With stories waiting to be told.
Yet every gust of wind, oh dear,
Tosses leaves, and lends an ear.

Chasing Dawn

Morning sunlight winks at me,
As branches stretch like limbs of glee.
A jogger trips on roots that spread,
Hoping the oak just shakes its head.

With boughs like arms that wave hello,
It mocks the sun, puts on a show.
Each dawn a prank, a giggling leaf,
That tickles time with disbelief.

The Harvest of Lost Seasons

Once a hipster acorn claimed,
His style was just too wild, untamed.
But when fall came, he rolled away,
Left resting squirrels in dismay.

Fall's bounty, laughter all around,
As leaves rain down without a sound.
The oak looks on, a stoic knight,
While squirrels argue over height.

Beneath the Elder's Canopy

Beneath this tree, we seek our muse,
But all we find are squirrel slews.
They're laughing loud at our confusion,
Claiming space with wild delusion.

The wise oak chuckles as we fumble,
While nutty plans begin to crumble.
We take a seat and roll our eyes,
Under a tree with secret skies.

A Life Written in Leaves

A poet's thoughts on bark engraved,
While passersby just misbehaved.
Laughter fills the air, so bright,
As winds whisper secrets in flight.

The tree's chronicler, leaf by leaf,
Winks and smiles, with playful belief.
Each leaf a page in nature's tome,
Where creatures halt and feel at home.

The Elder Tree's Final Whisper

In the yard, he stands so grand,
With mossy beard, and leaves unplanned.
He sways his branches, gives a wink,
What secrets in those rings, you think?

The squirrels plot their next grand feast,
While birds throw parties, not the least!
He often sighs with gentle grace,
'You kids are making quite the mess of space!'

Once he whispered to a breeze,
'Is life just holding up with ease?'
With each season, he cracks a joke,
'I'm still the king, and you're just smoke!'

As autumn paints his leaves with flair,
He shakes his limbs; can you hear the blare?
His laughter rings through every bough,
'You think I'm old? Just check the crowd!'

Chronicles of the Ancient Oak

Each ring a story, each knot a tale,
Of squirrels with acorns their ships set sail.
He mimics a pirate, with leafy hat,
'Yo ho, mateys! Where's the treasure at?'

When thunderstorms rumble, he's quite the fuss,
'These raindrops weigh more than my whole bus!'
Lightning may flash, but he stands so bold,
'I'll take your shocks - I'm old, not sold!'

The kids come running when summer is ripe,
'Let's build a fort, then start an all-night hype!'
He wears their laughter like a soft crown,
'Just don't let my bark get worn down!'

As seasons change and the winds do flip,
He brags of a thousand branches, none a drip.
He shakes a leaf and shouts with glee,
'Who needs a haircut? Just look at me!'

A Tapestry of Time and Shade

In a park where people stroll and play,
He waves his branches—'Come hang out, hey!'
With a tree trunk thick, he stands so near,
Razzmatazz, he says, 'I've got no fear!'

His shadows dance on the grass below,
As children giggle and run to and fro.
He's the original cool, with wisdom so vast,
'There's no need to rush; life's more fun slow cast.'

When the winds sing, he sways with style,
He rolls with the breeze for every mile.
His leaves applaud with a rustling cheer,
'Bring on the storms, I have no fear!'

So here's to the oak with bark worn and wise,
Making mischief beneath sunny skies.
He'll stand through the ages, still full of glee,
'Just don't ask my age— I'm ageless, you see!'

Reverberations of Earthbound Memories

In the shade of giants, laughs ensue,
Squirrels throw acorns like they're a zoo.
With each thud and bump, the ground shakes,
Nature's own comedy, no room for mistakes.

Branches wave gently, oh what a prank,
A bird on a branch gives a cheeky skank.
Echoes of giggles ring through the leaves,
As the old oak chuckles, "What a time to grieve!"

Whispers of woodland jesters we hear,
Embracing the moments that bring us cheer.
With every rustle, let laughter resound,
In the heart of the forest, fun knows no bound.

Oh mighty oak, wear your age with a jest,
You're the wise old fool, truly the best!
Sharing your tales of years gone by,
Telling us all: "Look up and fly!"

The Acorn's Journey to Grandeur

Once a small acorn, in mud did it sprout,
Dreaming of greatness, what's life all about?
Wiggling and giggling beneath the blue sky,
"If I were a tree, I'd reach up high!"

On a windy day, with a giddy little spin,
It danced through the forest, let the fun begin!
Every twist and turn brought cheers from the leaves,
"Soon I'll be mighty, just wait and believe!"

Grew taller and stronger, oh what a sight,
Shaking off squirrels who challenged its might.
"Hey there," it chuckled, "you can't have my hat!"
With a flick of a branch, it sent them off flat!

Now a grand oak, with a crown full of style,
Recalling the journey that took quite a while.
From tiny beginnings, it swings with delight,
An acorn once small is now quite the sight!

Roots Deep in Forgotten Dreams

Roots delve deep where the old secrets sleep,
In the arms of the earth, treasures to keep.
Whispers of dreams and giggles of yore,
Binding the history, a folklore galore.

"What's that?" asked the fern with a curious glance,
"Is it true you once joined a mossy dance?"
"Oh, indeed!" laughed the oak, with a wink and a grin,
"In my younger days, I had quite the spin!"

With roots wrapped around ages long past,
Funny old tales, and stories that last.
"Did you know," said a beetle with pride,
"I raced with the wind — but boy, I was fried!"

Through layers of laughter, buried dreams lie,
In a patch of soft grass under the blue sky.
Old oak and the fern keep those dreams alive,
In root's embrace, where we all can thrive.

Secrets Held in Whispering Foliage

Hidden in leaves, under branches so wide,
Laughter blends softly, like moss on the side.
The wind tells the tales of the tree and its friends,
Secrets of mischief that never quite ends.

"Oh, shh!" coos the crow, as it settles to hear,
"Did you catch the drake that danced with no fear?"
"Oh yes!" laughs the oak, "It tripped over a root,
And landed smack dab where it thought it could scoot!"

Foliage giggles at every old jest,
Whispers of wonder that time can't unquest.
Every rustle a reminder, life's funny and bright,
In the embrace of the oak, wrong feels so right.

As the sun dips low, shadows dance on the ground,
Laughter blooms freely, joy lightly bound.
In this green tapestry, secrets entwine,
Under the willow, the world feels divine!

Breath of the Winds Through Leaves

The breeze tickles the branches high,
Leaves laugh as they wave to the sky.
'What's the hurry?' they whisper, aflutter,
While squirrels wag tails, like a flirty butter.

Sunshine winks through the green above,
The tree grumbles, 'This is my love!'
Roots deep in the ground, oh what a feat,
'Can you lend me a hand?' they shout to our feet!

The twigs shimmy and sway to the tune,
'You can't catch us, we dance 'til noon!'
With every gust, a new joke unfurls,
The giggles exchange between leaves and pearls.

So next time you stroll by this ancient sage,
Stop for a moment, share a laugh and engage.
For in the winds and the rustling grounds,
Lies a world of chuckles, where humor abounds.

Tales Traced in the Dance of Bark

Picture a tale on this gnarled bark,
Written in scrawls like a quirky mark.
A squirrel's mischief, a thief of a nut,
Is etched on the oak, oh what a strut!

Woodpeckers knock, but not for a house,
"Why don't you try it? Get quiet as a mouse!"
Each peck resonates like a knock on the door,
Listen closely; it's laughter galore!

The knots in the wood bear stories untold,
Of breezy days when life was bold.
'Once I was slim, but I've grown a bit wide,
Now look at me; I've got nowhere to hide!'

So next time you peek at my resilient skin,
Know there's humor stitched deeply within.
With every crack and crevice so fine,
There's a story that tickles, and it's simply divine!

An Epic Written in the Silence

In silence I stand, my branches extended,
An epic unfolds, cheeky and splendid.
The whispers of history weave through the boughs,
While birds tell 'tales' as they sing their vows.

Oh what mischief is brewing above,
Is that a nest, or a feathered love?
Chirps and caws swirl as humor ignites,
A symphony of jest fills the crisp nights.

Starlit shadows play peekaboo games,
With moonlit echoes calling out names.
Each flicker of light births a chuckle, you see,
'Watch out for owls; they're judging your spree!'

So lean on my trunk, feel the giggles arise,
For in silence and stillness, humor flies.
Every bark and each leaf have secrets they tout,
Join in the laughter; let worries fade out!

Under the Watchful Gaze of Oak

Beneath my branches, squat and round,
The world spins swiftly with sights and sounds.
'What's that?' I hear, a rustle so near,
A cat gives a glance, it's time to disappear!

The leaves drop giggles, soft as a sigh,
As squirrels scold each other, 'Hey, that was my pie!'
The acorns roll 'round, all jolly and spry,
Playing dodgeball 'neath the vast azure sky.

Old tales are spun like sweet candy floss,
Of branches once strong now at a loss.
'Age is just numbers,' I chuckle with pride,
'Kings once sat here; they must've liked the ride!'

So come gather 'round, share a laugh or two,
Under my watchful gaze, with skies so blue.
Together we'll toast to the leaves and the lore,
In this jovial kingdom, there's always much more!

Song of the Timeless Guardian

In the forest, my limbs spread wide,
Squirrels gather, they cannot hide.
I'm their shadow, oh what a sight,
Their acorn stash, my little delight.

Birds chatter, holding a feast,
While woodpeckers tap, to say the least.
I stand tall, like a grand old chap,
While they squawk gossip, taking a nap.

My bark's a map, of many a year,
With stories hidden, but loud and clear.
Through seasons I've danced, laughed and cried,
A leafy jester, full of pride.

So swing by, dear friends, take a look,
At this wise fool, in nature's book.
Enjoy my shade, and share a laugh,
For life's a joke, not just a path.

Rustling Secrets of the Woodland

Whispers among my branches sway,
The critters conspire in silly play.
A raccoon smirks, with acorns stacked,
While rabbits giggle, and that's a fact.

As the winds blow, I dance with glee,
Leaves falling down like confetti, you see.
A caterpillar wiggles, wearing a hat,
Oh, trust me, I've seen much funnier than that!

The mushrooms chuckle, sprouting in rows,
While beetles strut, in their tiny shows.
I stand and watch, this grand charade,
Nature's circus, in hues that never fade.

So gather round, share in the cheer,
Join in the laughs, let go of fear.
For life here unfolds in delightful ways,
A rustling secret that never decays.

A Haven for Life's Fragile Threads

Beneath my branches, the world unfolds,
Tiny critters, with stories untold.
A spider spins, her web so bright,
While grasshoppers jump, full of delight.

A chipmunk hops, trying to pose,
While a ladybug flaunts her bright clothes.
They banter about who can jump high,
With laughter that tickles the clear blue sky.

Bees bumble past, buzzing their song,
In this wondrous space, where we all belong.
Each tiny giggle, a thread in fabric,
Life's tapestry spins, funny and epic.

So if you're weary from the daily grind,
Come visit my haven, see what you find.
Together we'll weave, with joy and mirth,
A fragile thread that connects us to Earth.

An Elder's Watch Over the Wild

Oh, how I chuckle, with bark so wise,
Watching the antics, of critters that rise.
A fox tells tales of the moonlit night,
While bunnies hop, in a clumsy flight.

My roots are deep, yet my heart is light,
Holding secrets of daytime and night.
With every breeze, I listen close,
To tales of mischief, the wild ones boast.

The fauna prance, a wild parade,
In my embrace, a bond is made.
From towering deer to the swiftest hare,
I'm the jovial elder, watching with care.

Let laughter echo, through woods so grand,
Join in the folly, hand in hand.
For life is a jest, a whimsical ride,
With me as your guide, come, let's confide!

Echoes of the Woodland Elder

In the forest stands a tree,
With limbs so wide, a sight to see.
He swears he heard a squirrel shout,
"Don't shake the branches, I'm out!"

His acorns drop like wisdom's seeds,
Planting thoughts in woodland deeds.
Critters chuckle, tales unfold,
Of nutty visions, legends told.

When birds ask him about his past,
He says, "I've seen it all, and fast!"
Each fluttered wing and rustled leaf,
Adds to his quirky disbelief.

With every season, whimsical bends,
He's the tree that just won't end.
A trunk with charm, a crown of glee,
In nature's circus, he's the marquee!

The Majestic Watcher

Oh mighty oak, you're quite the chap,
With limbs that wave and take a nap.
You snooze through storms, the rain, the sun,
While critters run, just having fun.

Your bark's a map of tales so funny,
Where chipmunks dance for acorn money.
A woodpecker's knocking at your door,
Are you awake, or just a bore?

Squirrels plot heists on your sturdy base,
While rabbits play a stealthy chase.
You watch with wisdom, though your roots,
Desire to join in their cute pursuits.

In alignment with the breeze, you stay,
The silent joker of the day.
If trees could laugh, yours would be loud,
For all the woodland's wacky crowd.

Veins of Life Through Weathered Wood

Beneath your bark, life's whims reside,
In veins of laughter, joy, and pride.
Tales unfold of when you were small,
Now you're a giant, the pride of all.

Your leaves are wrinkled, oh so wise,
Do you remember those butterfly flies?
Or the mishaps of a clumsy crow,
That tried to land on your boughs, oh no!

A spider spins jokes in a silken thread,
As you chuckle and nod your head.
The sun beams down, it's all a jest,
In this woodland, you're the best!

Your roots talk secrets under the ground,
With whispers of laughter all around.
Oldest oak, you bravely stand,
As the life of this wooded land.

Stories Woven in Green Shadows

In shadows green where stories dance,
You weave your tales, give life a chance.
The rabbits giggle, the mice all cheer,
For every acorn's a tale we hear.

Old knobby limbs with funny flair,
You grunt and groan, like you don't care.
Yet every laugh, and every snort,
Makes you the king of woodland court!

A breeze will sway, and leaves will rustle,
As creatures gather in a playful hustle.
From dusk till dawn, the fun's in store,
With you, dear oak, we all want more!

So when we speak of you today,
Know you're the heart of our woodland play.
An ancient sage, a jester too,
In every leaf, we laugh with you.

Timeless Roots in Silent Soil

In a meadow, wide and bright,
Stands a tree that's quite a sight.
Its roots are tangled, like a prank,
Trying to trip the passing tank.

Its branches wave like silly hands,
Grabbing clouds, making demands.
Whispers secrets to the breeze,
While squirrels plot with acorn keys.

The birds all laugh, they're part of the show,
With songs of woe from long ago.
The oak just grins, with ancient glee,
Guess it's hard to age when you're a tree!

When storms blow by, it sways with might,
Pretending it's a dance-off night.
But as it ages, a little stooped,
It dreams of being taller, then gets grouped.

The Sentinel of Seasons Past

There stands a guardian, strong and bold,
  Whose stories, like its bark, unfold.
  It puts the 'old' in old-time fun,
  With bark like wrinkles in the sun.

The squirrels gather, quite the show,
To steal its acorns, running fast, though.
"It's my treasure!" the oak shouts loud,
  But they just giggle, oh so proud!

A shadow large, a shade so sweet,
  Where picnics often claim their seat.
  It wonders if humans get tired,
  Of sitting round while it's so wired.

And when the leaves decide to drop,
  They twirl and dance, a leafy flop.
The oak just sighs, "Here we go again,
  As if my drops won't cause a 'trend'!"

Where Leaves Remember Time

A whisper drifts from every leaf,
Of gossip, laughter, joy, and grief.
Each flutter tells a joke or two,
Of times it rained and how it grew.

On windy days, they'd all compete,
To see who's fastest in retreat.
The oak just chuckles with dry bark,
"Keep coming back, this is quite the lark!"

In autumn's glow, a final cheer,
As colors clash in end-of-year.
It rolls its eyes at vibrant hues,
"Not my fault you snoozed on the news!"

When winter comes, oh boy, what fun!
Each flake of snow is a chilly stun.
It wears a coat, though slightly tight,
And dreams of summers filled with light.

A Canopy of Forgotten Tales

Underneath this grand old frame,
Lies a history, isn't it lame?
Of fairies lost, and goblins too,
Who'd wear shoes of morning dew.

The branches stretch, a jumpy stage,
For bugs who put on a circus page.
Each leaf holds secrets, wild and grand,
But mostly, food plots for the band.

In storms it huffs, it puffs, it sighs,
As lightning paints the gloomy skies.
"Bring it on!" it barks with pride,
While birds take shelter, coat-hiding inside.

Then once the calm returns with grace,
The oak just smiles, the quiet face.
In playful glee, it reminisces
"Who needs the past? Here's where the fun is!"

Roots Deep in Forgotten Earth

In the earth, your roots do play,
Finding lost socks from yesterday.
You sway and creak with such great glee,
Whispering secrets to bumblebees.

Each time the wind comes by to tease,
You dance like you're in a breeze.
But let's be honest, it's quite the show,
When branches wiggle, to and fro.

With acorns dropping, oh what a mess,
You drop your treats without any stress.
A squirrel's delight, a nutty spree,
Sharing your bounty, oh can't you see?

Old friend, you stand through rain and sun,
A wooden giant, just having fun!
Your humor's deep, just like your roots,
Life's a joke, and you bear the fruits.

Leaves Beneath the Gentle Sky

Leaves of gold and green that fall,
Carpet the ground, a nature ball.
You rustle softly, laugh a bit,
As kids make piles, and jump, they split!

A gust of wind, they dance and twirl,
Like nature's confetti, a joyful swirl.
"Oh no!" they shout, "the leaves attack!"
As they dive right into the leafy stack.

With every flutter, a giggling sound,
Echoes of fun all around.
You shade us from the sun's bright light,
While kids play hard, filled with delight.

Yet when it's time for winter's chill,
You stand bare, with a winter thrill.
But come spring, with new buds to sport,
You'll wear green again and start the report!

Echoes of the Silent Grove

In the quiet grove, secrets unfurl,
As whispers of nature start to twirl.
You stand like a keeper with tales to share,
While critters gather, as if in a fair.

A squirrel's chitter, a bird's sweet song,
Mix with your laughter, all day long.
"Is that a tree talking? No way, it's true!"
The forest giggles; the echo is you!

With each creak and groan, it's quite the jest,
As branches wave hello and take a rest.
Lost in your stories, oh what a thrill,
When little bugs dance, time seems to stand still.

So, let's celebrate this funny old place,
With laughter resounding, a warm embrace.
In your mighty presence, all cares fade,
The secret's out, it's a jolly parade!

Wisdom in Each Gnarled Knot

With gnarled knots, you've got the flair,
'Wisdom' written all over the air.
Wrapped in stories of laughter and cheer,
"Did you hear that? It's the wise one here!"

Covered in moss, like a fuzzy hat,
Who knew you'd get fashion tips like that?
Philosophy's branch, with a wink of glee,
You ponder life's questions while sipping tea.

"Why did the squirrel cross the road?" you ask,
"To stash another acorn, that's his task!"
Your humor runs deep, like roots in the ground,
As wise old leaves fall and spin all around.

So here's to you, the comic sage,
Defining humor with each passing age.
In every twist, a laughter's embrace,
You teach us all in this leafy space!

Where Legends Are Rooted

In a park where squirrels play,
An ancient oak stands tall today.
With branches wide like arms outspread,
It watches over all, well-fed.

Legends whispered in the breeze,
Of acorns that brought kings to knees.
With bark like wrinkles on a face,
It tells of time in every case.

It's seen romances bloom and fade,
And picnics where no one was paid.
The wise old tree just shakes his leaves,
And chuckles at all that he sees.

So throw a blanket, grab a snack,
Under the oak, there's no lack.
With roots that hold the tales we share,
Let's raise a toast to great old air!

The Path Beneath the Wide Boughs

With branches swaying, dance a jig,
A place where squirrels plot and dig.
The path beneath a leafy throne,
Where laughter echoes, never lone.

Old branches creak with every smile,
As visitors all stop awhile.
A throne of leaves for kings and fools,
In the shade is where no one drools.

The funky winds make stories twist,
Of beetles and of ants that missed.
Beneath this oak, the world's a show,
With plotlines that only trees know.

So gather round, let wishes fly,
Under the old oak's watchful eye.
Where paths are tangled, fun is found,
Together here, let joy abound!

A Testament of Strength and Grace

An old oak stands with style and grace,
Its trunk a monument to space.
With limbs that curve like grand parade,
It offers shade, but none are paid.

Its wisdom flows like honeyed tea,
Sharing tales of what used to be.
Of silly squirrels chasing dreams,
And pats from kids with giggly screams.

The seasons change, it rolls with flair,
With every leaf, a story rare.
Standing proud in sun and rain,
A tree that laughs through all the pain.

So tip your hat to strength and fun,
In nature's realm, it's number one.
For time may bend, but never break,
Here's to the tree—let's prance and shake!

Threads of Time in Every Leaf

In every leaf, a tale unfolds,
Of children's dreams and secrets told.
A rustle here, a giggle there,
An old oak listens with great care.

The wind tells jokes from days gone past,
As shadows dance and summer's fast.
Each knot and twist a laugh, a tear,
In every branch, there's nothing near.

When storms roll in, the tree stands firm,
With every gust, it sways and turns.
And when the sun breaks through the clouds,
It shouts out joy, and cheers the crowds.

So gather 'round this leafy friend,
Where stories start, and never end.
In every whisper, every swirl,
The oak rejoices, oh what a world!

The Mighty Guardian of Green

In the park where kids do play,
Stands a tree that steals the day.
With branches wide and leaves that sway,
He watches squirrels skedaddle away.

Old and wise, he cracks a grin,
As acorns drop like plump little sin.
A throne for birds, their feathered kin,
With every ache, he lets the fun begin!

His bark is rough, like nature's art,
Each knot and gnarled twig, a crucial part.
But with a smile, he steals our heart,
The laughter echoes, he plays his part!

So here's to him, our leafy friend,
In summer's warmth or winter's lend.
With every season, he will tend,
To tales of old, that never end.

Shadows Dance in the Sunlight

Beneath the shade, we gather round,
Where whirling shadows prance on ground.
The tree, our jester, looks so proud,
In leafy laughter, he's quite loud!

With every gust, a twirl, a spin,
His limbs a stage for birds to win.
And laughter spills like juice from skin,
While bees buzz sweet, joining in the din.

"Hey, watch that branch!" a kid will shout,
As acorns tumble all about.
The tree just chuckles without doubt,
Making us smile, as we flit about.

In sunny gleam, we find our fun,
The ancient oak, he's never done!
We bask beneath, till day is done,
In his embrace, we laugh, we run.

Tapestry Woven by Time

Lines and grooves like stories told,
Every ring a tale of old.
Underneath, the secrets bold,
Are whispered softly, never scrolled.

He's seen it all, the highs and lows,
From roaring storms to feathery snow.
With each new sprout, his wisdom grows,
In nature's dance, he steals the show.

"Hey, who's that critter?" kids will gasp,
As a raccoon peeks out to clasp.
The tree just chuckles, never a rasp,
"For all your tricks, I'm here to clasp!"

So gather 'round, let stories weave,
Of laughter shared on autumn leaves.
In this great bark, our joy retrieves,
A tapestry that never grieves.

A Tribute to Resilience's Form

With every season, he takes a bow,
Through wind and rain, he shows us how.
The kids all shout, "He's the big wow!"
For such great things, he won't allow!

"Hey, keep it down!" the neighbors yell,
As laughter rings out, sweet as a bell.
Yet he just sways, all is quite well,
In this grand show, he casts his spell.

From whimsical leaves to knobby roots,
He's dressed in green, with snazzy boots.
The laughter bubbles, joy never hoots,
As he dons laughs like festive toots!

A champion true, in shade and sun,
He gives us space to just have fun.
In his embrace, no need to run,
For in his shade, there's always one!

The Solace of Stalwart Stems

In a forest disco, the oak shakes a limb,
Leaves twist and turn, getting groovy on whim.
Squirrels run wild, planning wild, nutty pranks,
With acorn confetti, they show their thanks.

Old trunk with a smile, caught in a dance,
Roots tap the ground, oh what a romance!
Moss-covered shoes in this leafy soiree,
Who knew trees partied in such a way?

Branches tell tales of grandeur and sass,
Of storms they've survived and the critters they've amassed.
It's not just the wood, but the stories they tell,
Of rock and roll nights where the branches rebel.

So raise a toast to the foliage, oh so spry,
In this woodland carnival, where laughter flies high.
With every soft rustle and every nutty joke,
Let's celebrate together, our dear solid oak.

A Portrait of Time Under the Stars.

Beneath the night sky, our oak strikes a pose,
Dressed in moonlight, a celebrity who knows.
With starlight as glitter and the breeze as a fan,
Even the owls are fans of this plan.

Fireflies twinkle in a jealous glow,
While branches sway gently to music from below.
It buzzes with whispers from seasons gone past,
Each laugh and each tear, in its rings held fast.

Bark has its stories, like songs in a bar,
Of love and of loss that have traveled so far.
Its roots dive deep into history's embrace,
Sipping on wisdom, it still keeps the pace.

So crowd 'round the trunk, let's map every star,
And listen to secrets of what makes it bizarre.
For every old leaf holds a dance or a quirk,
And under this atlas, no one goes berserk.

Whispers of Ancient Bark

The oak confesses with a creak and a sigh,
"I've seen every fashion from twiglet to tie.
Fads come and go, from the nuts to the leaves,
But I keep it classic, with style that deceives."

The winds carry gossip from far and near,
The trees roll their eyes at the trends they hold dear.
"Remember that time when we danced in a blast?
I think it was spring, though it felt like the last!"

With critters who chat and the mushrooms who sway,
This trunk has opinions — and hey, they play!
Do you think I'm looking good with this weathered bark?

Just wait till next fall, I'll outshine the dark!"

So laugh with the shade, let the branches sway free,
Join in the banter with the wise oak tree.
It's not just an old tree, it's wisdom on show,
And chuckles galore in the belly below.

Guardians of the Grove

In the grove of giggles, the old oak stands tall,
Waving his branches, inviting us all.
With roots intertwined like buddies that chill,
Squirrels take selfies, what a viral thrill!

A wise old sentinel with mossy-gray hair,
He watches the critters in their joyous affair.
From deer prancing lightly to raccoons in masks,
Each moment a treasure, each day wears new tasks.

Knotty and knobby, he grins with delight,
As dance parties erupt in the cool of the night.
Leaves rustle laughter, as the owl takes a twirl,
With a wink to the moon, watch the fun unfurl.

These guardians of laughter cherish each jest,
Creating a kingdom where fun is the quest.
So let's give a cheer for the oak and its crew,
In this grove of giggles, there's always room for you!

The Oak's Quiet Resilience

In the corner of the park, he stands tall,
His branches whisper secrets, a wise old pal.
Squirrels throw acorns, with not much grace,
While birds share gossip, in a feathered race.

His trunk is a fortress, a grand old knight,
Fighting off storms, with all of his might.
And though he's a bit creaky, he won't complain,
He just smiles at the sunshine, like it's champagne.

Each year he grows taller, with a wink and a nod,
As kids climb his branches, to feel like a god.
"Keep your hands off my leaves!" he might jokingly say,
"But the view from up here, oh what a display!"

In the fall, he's a jester, a sight to behold,
With his golden curls, he shimmers like gold.
So here's to the oak, with his quirky old charm,
He shelters us all, keeping us safe from alarm.

Old Friend of the Sky and Soil

He's the type of tree that tells bad jokes,
Like why did the leaf never stop to smoke?
Because it was afraid of a little hot air,
But he's too rooted; he doesn't have a care!

With branches outstretched, waving at the sun,
His bark is slightly rough, but oh what fun!
When folks sit beneath, they giggle and sigh,
At his wrinkled old face, that looks up to the sky.

"Did you hear the one about the acorn?" he'll crow,
"Why did it go to school? To become a tree, you know!"
As laughter echoes, the forest joins in,
His leafy crown sways, wearing the grin.

So lift up your glasses, here's raising a toast,
To the old friend who stands, watching us the most.
With his roots in the ground and quirks galore,
He makes nature's theater, a playful encore.

Where Nature's Heart Beats Strong

In the heart of the woods, where the creatures play,
Lives a wise old oak who thinks he's the 'heyday'.
With a trunk full of stories and leaves full of glee,
He waves to the winds, "Come dance close to me!"

When autumn arrives, it's a colorful spree,
With leaves falling down like confetti from a tree.
He giggles and rumbles, "Isn't this grand?
Just look at my wardrobe, isn't it well planned?"

The critters all gather, in his shady embrace,
While critiquing his bark, they decide it's a race.
"First one to the top gets to sing the loud song,"
The branches shake softly, "Join in, come along!"

The forest erupts in a raucous delight,
As nuts fall down laughing, the pine trees unite.
With each passing season, his humor stays strong,
For the heart of nature beats where fun walks along.

The Sheltered Soul of the Forest

Beneath the old oak, the children all play,
He watches them closely, in his slow, wise way.
With a laugh he declares, "My shade's quite the hit,
But don't climb too high; you might fall, just a bit!"

He's a storyteller grand, with treasures to share,
Of seasons and critters, both here and up there.
"Life's just like me, all twisted and free,
Embrace every twist, let your heart be a tree!"

The leaves start to chuckle when the wind softly blows,
As they swirl in a dance, like a troupe of grand toes.
"Take a chance!" they say, "Get lost in the breeze,
For with every gust, the adventure's a tease!"

So here's to the oak, our jovial friend,
May his humor and strength never come to an end.
With laughter and shade, he's a treasure so rare,
The soul of the forest, in his comforting care.

The Heartbeat of the Forest

In a clearing where the sunbeams lay,
An old oak tree steals the show each day.
With limbs outstretched like a dance of glee,
It whispers secrets, just between you and me.

Its acorns drop like little bombs,
Squirrels plot heists with tiny qualms.
They scamper and chatter, plotting their fate,
But the old oak just laughs, 'Oh, you're too late!'

Birds make a ruckus, a feathery crew,
Perched on its branches, they think they're so cool.
They sing off-key, but it sways with pride,
The grand old oak basks in nature's wild ride.

With roots so deep it knows every tale,
From picnics gone wrong to a stormy gale.

Legends Carved in Knotted Grain

Etched in bark are the tales of old,
Of daring squirrels and acorns bold.
A heart carved there says, 'Lovers unite!'
But surely, they laughed when things didn't go right.

Fungi and moss throw wild parties, too,
Whole clubs of insects that party for you.
The gossip runs deep from root to the sky,
'Who made that mess? Was it him or a fly?'

A raccoon sometimes strolls, tiptoes like a thief,
Raiding the snack bowls, it's a real mischief.
The oak just shakes, and its leaves all chuckle,
While raccoon in belly, gives a little rustle.

As tales unfold in the aging wood,
With laughter and songs, it feels mighty good.

Dance of the Wind Through Boughs

The breezy jig through the leaves up high,
Twisting and twirling with a bump and a sigh.
Each gust a dancer, frolicking around,
While the oak stands steady, glad for the sound.

A hawk swoops close; it thinks it can lead,
But the old oak smiles, 'I'm planted, take heed!'
'You soar on the wind, but I stand my ground,
In this forest waltz, I will always be found.'

A gentle breeze tickles the bark's rough face,
The whispers of laughter spread through the space.
The oak and the wind share this playful dance,
Creating a moment that's pure happenstance.

So come join the fun in the sun's golden rays,
Let the laughter linger for all of your days.

The Wisdom of a Thousand Rings

With every ring, a memory grows,
From tiny seeds to the stormy throes.
It chuckles softly as time flows free,
Watch out, young saplings, it winks with glee!

Each year it sways, all wise and aloof,
The young trees whisper, 'Is that our proof?'
A trunk so thick, like a history tome,
It shares its wisdom—the forest is home.

So, gather round and listen close,
For every gust brings the oak's grandiose prose.
The laughter of nature, so merry and bright,
Keeps our spirits high, in the afternoon light.

So here's to the oak, with its snickers and grins,
In the heart of the woods, where the fun never thins.

Whispers of the Ancient Boughs

Old oak stands tall, with hair quite gray,
Branches like arms in a wild ballet.
Squirrels on branches, they chatter and tease,
While birds make their nests, the old fella sneezes!

A family gathering, acorns abound,
"Watch your hats, folks!" the old oak has found.
With each gust of wind, a leaf takes to flight,
"Oh dear, looks like dinner's blown out tonight!"

Sentinel of Seasons Past

The old oak shrugs as seasons pass by,
"Again with the snow? Oh my, oh my!"
In summer, it boasts, "Look at my shade!"
But drops the gossip when autumn's displayed.

Leaves crackle and whisper, a rustling song,
This old tree wonders, "How can I last so long?"
Time ticks away, with each ring a laugh,
"Just don't ask about my tree-age graph!"

The Heartwood's Secret

Deep in the trunk, secrets lie thick,
Like the jokes of a bard, some take time to tick.
When asked about wisdom, it gets quite coy,
"I'm just a big fella who loves a good ploy!"

Raccoons gather round, with tales to exchange,
"Last winter was wild, but this year is strange!"
Yet the heartwood chuckles, as leaves swish about,
"Life's just a riddle, my friends, there's no doubt!"

Embrace of the Timeless Canopy

Up in the branches, the critters convene,
Planning their mischief while staying unseen.
"Let's prank the humans!" the squirrel did shout,
Old oak just chuckled, "What's that all about?"

Through wind and through storms, it rocks with delight,
"Bring it on, nature! I'll stand and I'll fight!"
Yet when it's all quiet, it hums a soft tune,
"Who needs a crown when you've got the moon?"

Echoes in the Canopy Above

In the branches, whispers play,
Squirrels giggle night and day.
Owls who hoot like they own the place,
Wonder if they'll win the race.

The leaves are having quite a chat,
Telling tales of this and that.
One says, 'I'm the best of green!'
Another laughs, 'Have you been seen?'

Shadows dance upon the ground,
Jumping squirrels, round and round.
If old trees could only laugh,
They'd bust a gut on nature's path.

The oldest oak, he rolls his bark,
While birds chirp songs that hit the mark.
With each breeze, a funny jolt,
As acorns drop, they serve the volt.

The Leader of the Woodland Assembly

Gather 'round the old oak tree,
It's the place to be, you see!
Beneath his limbs, the creatures meet,
Debating if acorns taste sweet.

The rabbits hop, the foxes prance,
While owls stare like they've got a chance.
The old oak smiles, branches wide,
'Let's vote! Who thinks the ground hogs lied?'

Squirrels raise their tiny paws,
Chirping loudly their own cause.
Even the ants chime in for fun,
Counting acorns—oh, what a run!

Yet in the end, with a creaky moan,
The oak declares, 'I'll stand alone!'
For in this wood, he's king by birth,
Though never enters a debate of worth.

Guardians of the Green Universe

Beneath a crown of tangled leaves,
The critters plot, as nature weaves.
'Who's guarding what?' a raccoon said,
'The trees, the bugs, or the "wormy" bread?'

The old oak laughs, a hearty sound,
'Guardians? We're just hanging around!'
The birds squawk truths with no real clue,
As they debate the sky's deep blue.

Groundhogs whisper, hide and seek,
While bumbles sway and softly squeak.
The mushrooms cheer, they're full of spunk,
In the green universe, it's all just funk!

So raise a leaf in raucous cheer,
For even trees can crack and leer.
In this grand forest, so cleverly free,
The guardians? Oh, they're just goofy debris!

The Old One's Soliloquy

What tales do I hold in this gnarled trunk?
Of squirrels who think they're really punk.
   'Watch me climb!' they boast with flair,
     While I just stand, like I don't care.

The birds think they're the next pop stars,
   While ants are aiming for tiny cars.
   'Why don't you fly?' I often tease,
But their feet stay rooted in search of cheese!

   With every breeze, I sway and creak,
     As if the wind has secrets to leak.
     Yet here I stand, wise and bleak,
   Observing the folly, week after week.

So here's to the minions beneath my shade,
   In this leafy circus, I've been unmade.
Remember, dear friends, as you climb and shout,
   I'm the old grump, but I'm watching out!

www.ingramcontent.com/pod-product-compliance
Lightning Source LLC
Chambersburg PA
CBHW051638160426
43209CB00004B/708